Stephen Mason Merrill

The organic Union of American Methodism

Stephen Mason Merrill

The organic Union of American Methodism

ISBN/EAN: 9783743332058

Manufactured in Europe, USA, Canada, Australia, Japa

Cover: Foto ©ninafisch / pixelio.de

Manufactured and distributed by brebook publishing software (www.brebook.com)

Stephen Mason Merrill

The organic Union of American Methodism

THE ORGANIC UNION

OF

AMERICAN METHODISM.

BY BISHOP S. M. MERRILL.

CINCINNATI: CRANSTON & STOWE.
NEW YORK: HUNT & EATON.
1892.

Copyright
By CRANSTON & STOWE,
1892.

INTRODUCTORY.

THE writer desires it understood that in the following pages he speaks for himself alone, and not for the Church in any sense whatsoever. No one is authorized to speak for the Church on the subject presented. Some will doubt the propriety of this publication, unofficial as it is; but, after weighing the matter as carefully as possible, the persuasion is clear that the things herein said ought to be said, and that the present time for saying them is as opportune as any likely to come in the near future.

It will be observed that he confines himself to his own views and impressions. He is not ignorant of the literature on the subject that accumulated in the years of controversy, but he passes it by in silence. No attempt is made to sustain or illustrate his positions by citations of authority. His purpose has been to set forth his thoughts in outline, with genuine frankness and plainness of speech, yet not in the way of controversy. It has been impossible to do this at some points without the appearance of argument, but he verily believes he has maintained fairness and indulged no feeling contrary to that which he commends to others. It is but just to say that he is not sanguine in the expectation of witnessing the desired consummation in his day; but he can not see in that fact any reason for withholding his convictions, or refusing to contribute whatever of influence his words may have towards the better understanding so certainly needed.

He entered the ministry the year the division of the Church occurred, and through a door indirectly opened as the result of division, and afterwards spent some years on the debated ground, often coming in contact with the bitterest feelings engendered in the strife on the border; so that his recollections of the old debates are vivid, and sometimes sad. In his ministry in the times of slavery he has met organized mobs in his congregations; has been arraigned before mass-meetings of regulators, with a view to his expulsion from the State; has been presented to the grand jury for indictment under special legislation designed to send him to the State's Prison; has been threatened with bludgeons, tar-buckets, and bullets; and, therefore, he does not forget the former days, when to represent the Methodist Episcopal Church on Southern soil was at once a peril and an honor. After all, he bears no ill-feeling towards Southern people or Churches, but wishes and prays, not only for fraternity, but also for ultimate organic union.

While the latter may be delayed, the time is at hand for something more than Conference fraternity. There ought to be practical union and co-operation in foreign missionary work. There is no need of a divided Methodism in China, Japan, or Mexico. It is a reproach to us if a plan for this can not be devised. In this country there should be provision for the easier transfer of preachers from one Church to the other. Men and families in the South need the benefit of the climatic change to a higher latitude. Useful lives might be prolonged. Some whose health will not stand the rigor of Northern winters could work efficiently in the Southern States. There are more in this condition than our work in the South will accommodate. As things now are, such changes require withdrawal from the Church, and some risk and uncertainty in gaining admission. The bishops could easily concur in transfers between the Churches, if authorized by their respective General Conferences. In several respects it is possible to improve the relations of the Churches, in a practical way, without consolidation. Let all pray for divine guidance.

CHICAGO, December, 1891.

ORGANIC UNION.

I.

THE subject of the future relations of the dissevered branches of the Methodist family is sufficiently important to attract attention to the utterances of any one who feels moved to give expression to thoughts which have become convictions, especially when clothed in the language of moderation and sincerity.

The writer has convictions which are not the outgrowth of any suddenly awakened emotion; but which have been formed after careful observation of the situation of the Churches, and the best study he could give to all the elements of the problem. He is not a recent convert to the views he now holds. What he believes to-day he has believed for more than a score of years, and his convictions have grown with advancing life till a sense of duty impels him to say what he has hitherto cherished in his heart. He is aware that he says it at the risk of precipitating a discussion which has been postponed so long that it has become almost too delicate to be mentioned. There is room for differences of opinion with regard to the expediency of this discussion; yet there is scarcely a probability that the "convenient season" for beginning it will come at all, if all wait till every one is ready for it. If it were to be an angry controversy, or a discussion conducted otherwise than in the truest Christian spirit, it might be well to defer it as long as possible; but a calm inquiry into existing facts and conditions, with a view to ascertaining the exact truth in the premises, can not be hurtful to any interest of the Church, and certainly not to that growing spirit of fraternity which we all recognize and in which we delight.

By the union of Methodist Churches is meant the consolidation of all the denominations of Methodism in the United States in one governmental jurisdiction. "A wild, visionary idea," says one. "An impracticable scheme," says another. "Impossible and inexpedient," is the response of a multitude. These answers are anticipated, as they have all been given before; and yet it must not be overlooked that they cover the exact points of inquiry, and seek to dismiss the issue without so much as considering it. Against this summary way of dealing with questions of such deep significance, solemn protest is in order. Both the intelligence and the piety of the Church are impeached by it. If the result contemplated is in harmony with the spirit of the gospel, there can be no wisdom in pronouncing it an impossibility. "Whatever ought to be, can be," is a better maxim for those who believe the cardinal doctrines of Methodism.

To expect this grand consummation to be brought about without an effort, would be visionary indeed. Time, study, preparation, and sacrifice will all be required; and this, after the purpose has been formed to reach the end, as well as in the preliminary steps that lead to that purpose. He who fails to appreciate the magnitude of the undertaking is not prepared for the discussion of the subject, nor to sit in judgment on the issue when it is presented. No thoughtful person will look upon it as other than an enterprise of proportions equal to anything heretofore attempted in the history of religious denominations.

Perhaps the first point to be studied is the question which will arise in many minds as to whether the consolidation is really desirable. Some declare that it is not. If this opinion is conscientiously entertained by any considerable numbers, and represents a judgment formed after weighing the facts and principles involved, while it can not be conclusive as to the merits of the question, it is nevertheless entitled to respectful consideration. The reasons alleged in its support indicate the existence of apprehensions that so great a denomination would be liable to corruption; that it would lose the evangelical spirit; that it would be unable to maintain soundness of doctrine; that it would fail to enforce discipline, so as to uphold the proper standard of morality; that its fellowship would be sought by worldly men for unworthy ends; and, finally, that it would become a great political power, and prove dangerous to the liberties of the country. There is enough in these suggestions to cause hesitancy in adopting an opposite view; and yet it is not improbable that those who have concluded differently have already hesitated long enough to look into the face of the supposed dangers, and to see whatever of force or probability there is in them. It is well for those who still hesitate to inquire to what extent they are governed by worldly wisdom, and whether they give full play to their faith in the divine element in the gospel, and whether they recognize the providential agency in directing the affairs of the Church. Are we to conclude that the Church can only be kept true to her mission while she is small in numbers, weak in influence, and hampered with rivalries and competitions? Must she be rent into fragments in order to keep alive her evangelizing power? Is it necessary that she be torn with schisms in order to avoid cherishing heresies? Are we to believe that her ability to enforce the morality of the New Testament is limited to a small number of communicants? Did our Divine Redeemer mistake the conditions of human society when he prayed that his disciples might be one?

There is danger in this discussion, it is admitted, of falling into the illogical method of applying principles which belong to the spiritual household of faith to our denominational affairs. The Scriptural doctrine of the unity of the Church is easily interpreted in the spiritual sense. It is not claimed that the lines of our ecclesiastical structures can be made to quadrate with those of the kingdom of God. The "one fold" of the "one Shepherd" is larger than all the Methodisms in the world. This is freely conceded; yet unnecessary divisions of the Church are to be deplored. They tend to unhealthful rivalries, weakness, and waste of resources that ought to be conserved for the enhancement of religious power.

There has never been a division in Methodism that was not felt to be a calamity. In every instance the leaders in the movement resulting in division professed reluctance and sadness in going out. They thought it the last resort to secure redress of grievances or rights that were in jeopardy. They are entitled to credit for sincerity and good intentions. Then, it must be that, in the judgment of all parties, with all personal rights reasonably guaranteed, union is better than division. This is as true to-day as it has ever been. One great Church, with all the dangers that arise from its greatness, is better than any number of small Churches of the same doctrine and usages, comprising the same membership, and reaching the same communities. If division is deplorable, union is desirable. Fraternity means brotherhood, and wherever there is brotherhood enough to justify fraternal relations between Churches of the same faith and order, there is enough to justify and require the most strenuous efforts to remove divisions, and to establish that highest type of fraternity which most nearly expresses the spirit of unity for which all true disciples earnestly pray.

If unnecessary divisions of Methodism are to be deplored as calamities, as all concede, it can hardly be denied that the unnecessary continuance of old divisions, after the causes and occasions of division have been removed, is equally deplorable.

This statement is pivotal. It is purposely guarded. In it lies the essence of the great issue. What constitutes the "necessary" or "unnecessary continuance of old divisions?" It is conceivable that complications may arise after the division, which may render reunion difficult or undesirable, independently of all relations to the original causes of division. Have such complications arisen in any case, or with any of the Churches which have gone out from the original Methodism of America? This involves questions of fact, to be canvassed in studying the relations of particular Churches.

Possibly another question is antecedent to this. Have the causes of division been sufficiently removed to call for this question of subsequent complications? The categorical "yes" or "no" will not be a satisfactory answer; nor will the opinion of one who never believed there was any sufficient cause for division be accepted as of any weight. The historical review is indispensable. In case of the minor divisions it is brief. The first division on the slavery question occurred about a half century ago. It took out of the Methodist Episcopal Church some excellent people, whose extreme anti-slavery sentiments moved them to secede because they could not fellowship pro-slavery Church members. They formed the Wesleyan Connection. When slavery was abolished, many of the leaders of the body returned. They were cordially received. In their return no disparagement or dishonor followed them. This "Connection" adopted other principles at variance with the mother Methodism, but nothing involving questions of conscience. They opposed episcopacy, declared against secret societies, etc., and made quite a showing of differences. But the episcopacy which they condemned never existed in Methodism. Their zeal burned against prelacy, autocracy, and all Romanistic tendencies; but there is nothing in "our episcopacy" to merit the denunciations poured out upon such evils. In their differences from us with regard to episcopacy there is nothing but matters of opinion or preference—nothing whatever that can justify division. In our Church there has always been the largest liberty on the subject of secret societies. Some of our members belong to them, and others oppose them heartily. It has never been made a subject of ecclesiastical action. The Church binds no one's conscience in this respect, nor interferes with the liberty of members beyond the requirement of correctness of faith and life. It is therefore plain that there is no substantial reason for the continued existence of this small and uninfluential body of Methodists. The present generation knows very little of the old "radical" controversy which related to the formation of the Methodist Protestant Church. For many years it agitated Methodism through all her borders. The heat and bitterness attending it resulted more from the ardent temperaments of the men engaged in it than from the serious character of the issues involved. To us it now seems as if the points in dispute might have been considered dispassionately. The chief question related to lay representation. That is now a thing of the past. Lay representation came in time, and the unsettled details will be adjusted without friction. The Methodist Protestant body also became non-episcopal. Its opposition to the office of bishop was intense, not to say violent. The kind of episcopacy that called forth its severest anathemas existed only in the heated imaginations of those who gave to fancy's wing the largest freedom.

The administrative office as it exists, in fact, has but little in it that alarms the Methodist Protestants of to-day. At least it does not present a question of conscience. The attempt to build up a strong non-episcopal Methodist Church has had a fair trial, and has not been such an eminent success as to warrant a continuance or a repetition. There is scarcely room left for the pretense that Episcopal Methodism does not furnish all needed spiritual advantages to all who believe Methodist doctrines. Nor is there any reason why Methodists should fear oppression under her "rules and regulations." With a government strong enough to assume efficiency, and liberal enough to afford the fullest religious freedom to all communicants, she offers the gospel to all classes, and a spiritual home to all who desire to work out their salvation.

In addition to the Churches named, there are several other Methodist bodies in the country striving for a precarious existence, and endeavoring to do the work of Methodism in good earnest, it may be conceded, but under great disadvantages. The Free Methodists, the Primitive Methodists, and the Congregational or Independent Methodists, all have their differences, and especially their divergences from the Methodist Episcopal Church; but their differences are matters of opinion and preference merely, and not of such character as to involve conscience. It can not be that their separation from the great body of Methodists is essential to their happiness or to their advancement in grace; and certainly it can not be promotive of any interest of spiritual Christianity. If all who love the Lord could learn to allow conscience full play in the realm of morals, and never force it into the sphere of opinions—where there ought to be freedom—the cause of God and of Church unity would be greatly served.

This reference to the minor divisions is made for illustration, as well as to express an honest belief with regard to them. Their independence as Churches is unquestionably their right; but, in the present condition of religious knowledge, it is extremely difficult to justify their separate existence. There is nothing vital in any one of them that is not in the Methodist

Episcopal Church—in doctrine, discipline, spiritual life, or moral teaching. But the reader will anticipate correctly that the chief purpose of this writing is to consider the larger division of the Church—the sorest in Methodist history—and to study the question of reunion in relation to the Methodist Episcopal Church and the Methodist Episcopal Church, South. This is to be the burden of our theme, as it is the burden of many hearts in thought and prayer.

II.

IN the late Ecumenical Conference, when the subject of "co-operation" was under consideration, there were some expressions made in favor of the organic union of the different Methodisms. The strongest utterances came from representatives of the Methodist Episcopal Church. This was proper; for the oldest and strongest should first speak, and give encouragement to the others to follow.

It was noticeable that the representatives of the Methodist Episcopal Church, South, remained silent on that occasion, so far as organic union was concerned. From that silence, and from the comments afterward made in their papers, it is readily inferred that those in position to direct public sentiment in the Southern Church are opposed to the agitation of this subject. For years past there has been a studied effort on their part to avoid this discussion. They believe it unwise, and they are entitled to the freest exercise of their opinion without the slightest impeachment of their motives. They see things as some of us do not. We only ask that they permit us to differ from them as widely and as sincerely as they differ from us. But this permission involves a difficulty. The liberty we ask is to speak, when they prefer that we do not speak. In this we can not please them, and yet follow the behest of duty as that behest comes to us. Let it be understood, then, that we speak for ourselves only, and not for them. Indeed, as before said, this writer speaks for himself alone, and not in any sense for his Church.

There is little probability that organic union with the Methodist Episcopal Church, South, will ever be consummated without a pretty thorough sifting of the old issues. Can this be done without fighting the old battles over again? Is it possible to review the history of the division, and reach a common understanding of the facts, so as to lay the foundation for adjustment, without arousing the old passions and prejudices which played so large a part in the disruption? If the answer is negative, it proves nothing as to the merits of the case, but only that more time and grace are needed in order to meet the high obligation. With some of us it is a settled conviction that a candid discussion of honest differences between Christian people can be so conducted as to contribute to peace and harmony, rather than to strife and discord. If not, why not? What is our Christianity worth if it does not give us grace to do this thing?

Let us interpret the silence which has so long prevailed, and which some still insist upon maintaining. Does it mean that there is no feeling on the subject? Rather does it not mean that there is some intangible influence in the atmosphere of the Churches, manifested now and then in tentative questionings, which is producing beneath the surface a quiet growth of sentiment in favor of a better understanding between dissevered brethren? In the experience of pastors it has been found that where Church feuds have alienated brethren for a long time, the old enmities had died out before the parties were aware of it; that both had wearied of the estrangement, and desired reconciliation; that nothing was wanting but that each should be apprised of the feeling of the other party, and that as soon as this point was reached, the adjustment of differences was easy. There is no reason to doubt that substantially this condition of things exists among the members of the two branches of Methodism to-day. Whatever the feeling of the leaders, the people have no desire to perpetuate the alienation. Up to this time neither party has expressed its deepest convictions—probably because no one fully understands the sentiments of his neighbors; or it may be because no one has felt authorized to speak for the Church as a whole. Whatever the cause of the prevailing silence, the inference is not forced that the absence of discussion indicates the existence of a reserved conviction that the people need only leadership to induce them to demand the removal of the alienations of the past, and the restoration of genuine Methodist fellowship with all the branches of the Methodist family.

With the great mass of the membership of the Methodist Episcopal Church there is scarcely any consciousness of alienation. They have never entered into the old disputes, and have inherited no element of bitterness from the agitations which rent the body before they were active in Church-life. Not one in a thousand has the slightest prejudice to overcome in according to the members of the Southern Church the fullest recognition and fellowship. When their attention is called to it, they simply wonder why there is a Southern Church. It can be assumed, therefore, that our people are ready for the reunion whenever it shall be brought about; and it is equally true that they are not fretted because of the delay. They are in condition to look at the subject without bias, to take the broadest view that can be presented, and to act dispassionately and in the most catholic spirit. It is not improbable that a similar condition of things exists in large sections of the Southern Church. The members are in that Church because it is to them the Methodist Episcopal Church. In thought and feeling they are simply Methodists. Between them and our people there is no barrier to fellowship. Why should there be? The people never divided the Church. In all the agitations that led to the division, the people were scarcely heard. The preachers took the lead. They created prejudices in the minds of the people, and aroused evil passions in many of them, till they felt, as they wished to feel, that they had the people behind them. The preachers were responsible for the rupture, and they are responsible for the continuance of the opposition to reunion, so far as such opposition exists. To them belongs whatever of praise or blame should be awarded for the separate organization of Methodism. The preachers, in the pulpit and in the press, possess the means of promoting or of repressing discussion, and they are fully able to control popular sentiment in the Church. Hitherto they have not been slow to exercise this ability. When the time arrives to make an appeal in behalf of reunion, that appeal must be to the ministry, if it be effective, and not to the laity. What the preachers desire in this respect, they can secure. The people are right in heart. They look to the ministry for leadership and instruction, and follow gladly in all lines of religious activity and Christian fellowship. There is therefore no necessity for those in leading positions in the Church to await the movement of the people in the matter of discussing the desirability and the practicability of reunion.

It is easy to believe what one desires to believe. When convinced that reunion is desirable; that the old breach ought to be healed; that a united Methodism is better than a divided Methodism; that the consolidation would enhance the power of the Church, increase her facilities for doing good, and in every way conduce to the success of the ministry and the happiness of the people, the practical difficulties in the way of accomplishing the result will diminish with amazing rapidity. With both Churches anxious to come into the new relation, there would develop such skill in solving problems, and such readiness in devising schemes of adjustment, as to astonish those whose faith falters at the suggestion of so formidable an undertaking.

The fact is not overlooked that the consolidation would touch the episcopacy, the Book Concerns, the secretaryships, the editorships, and all Church boards. Corporations, vested rights, charters, wills, legacies, endowments, and numerous questions of titles and legal obligations will figure in the negotiations. It is not pleasant to suppose that the effect of the reunion on the prospects of official promotion will be a factor of any seriousness in a matter so far-reaching in spiritual results. Would that this thought might be dismissed altogether! But how can it be? Under the guise of a laudable ambition to be useful, preachers do aspire to occupy positions which will give them a wider field for the exercise of their abilities. They were either more or less than human if they did not. Sometimes the laudable and the selfish ambitions are scarcely distinguishable. It is possible that this very thought of official advancement will insinuate itself into some minds, and bias their judgments, even when they are unconscious of any selfish motives. In such cases the difficulties to be overcome will appear insuperable. Great as they are in fact, they will magnify themselves immeasurably to the fancy.

No effort should be made to ignore real difficulties. Whatever their nature, they should be studied in all their bearings. What is desired is not a patched-up truce, or a forced silence with reference to old enmities still rankling in the heart, but a genuine restoration of confidence and affection, the outcome of a thorough understanding. The first step toward the attainment of this end is a frank concession, each to the other, of motives worthy of high Christian character. It is not too much to assume that the time has come for this first step. Indeed, it has already been taken in the fraternity established. The parties stand side by side, upon equal ground, in brotherly relations, ready for the next step. That will be a rehearsal of the agreements and disagreements between the Churches, as an intelligent understanding of the differences to be adjusted can not be gained without a candid comparison of notes with reference to the whole field of controversy. When this can be done without passion or crimination, real progress will be made in the direction of consolidation. So long as we are unable to talk over the past without reviving the old animosities, the time is not here for the discussion, much less for the union.

As the difficulties to be overcome are neither few nor small, the warmest friends of the movement will be the most patient. No one will look for the consummation in a brief space of time. If it be accomplished within a generation, it may be accepted as an achievement of wise diplomacy and royal statesmanship, sustained by the noblest devotion to a cause which concerns the glory of God and the welfare of his kingdom. Impetuous zeal will retard, rather than hasten, the happy day. Before it dawns we shall have to look away from the human to the divine side of the question. The conviction must be wrought into our souls that God wills the reunion and will smile upon it. Then mountains will dwindle in the presence of a generous faith. Broad-mindedness is indispensable. Those who lead in the enterprise must be great enough to desire, above all earthly things, to bring Methodism into closer harmony with God's gracious purpose respecting the future of his kingdom.

While men yet linger who know the history of the rupture, and can remember the chief actors in the contest, is the proper time to begin the agitation looking to the healing of wounds which must be healed ere the full-orbed sun of prosperity shines upon Methodism, girded to fill the measure of her providential mission.

There is only one source of apprehension concerning this discussion. It is that overzealous partisans on either side may rush into it with imperfect knowledge of the facts, and say things in haste which were better never said. Sad if passion should get the start of reason. Men of narrow views and selfish feelings can easily prove themselves efficient as obstructionists. These are to be dreaded. But the wiser counsels will prevail in the end. There is a future to this Methodism of ours which reaches into the millenniums. Men of wisdom and faith look to that long future in planning the work of to-day. They see in it verified promises of the divine blessing in conquests and consummations exceeding all the calculations of the timid. They look for a future of toil and sacrifice indeed, but for triumphs more glorious than any yet achieved.

Let Christian men reason together as Christian men should, and let them look hopefully for the blessings a united Methodism will bring;

and, after the clouds of doubt and discord shall have passed away, will be seen the tardy feet of truth walking the highway of peace, and in her train all needed concessions, mutual respect, and ultimate oneness.

III.

THE study of the relations of the two Churches since the division brings the conclusion that the duty of initiating negotiations looking to formal fraternity devolved properly upon the Methodist Episcopal Church. This grew out of the proceedings of the General Conference of 1848, as well as out of the fact that she is the original body from which the other separated, and therefore, in the technical sense at least, the offended party. Ever since the General Conference at Pittsburg declined to receive the fraternal delegate sent to it from the Methodist Episcopal Church, South, all have conceded that the next step in that direction should be taken by the parent body. Recognizing this fact, and feeling impressed that some advances should be made, two representative men of the Church, in 1870, voluntarily made a friendly visit to the General Conference of the Methodist Episcopal Church, South. That visit, although entirely informal and unofficial, produced quite a sensation in Church circles at the time. The distinguished visitors— Bishop Janes and Rev. W. L. Harris, D. D.— were treated with personal consideration becoming their rank, but the visit itself was less kindly received than might have been expected. While it produced no immediate result, and was severely criticized as if of a semi-official character, it was, nevertheless, the occasion of a correspondence which led to the establishment of fraternal relations between the Churches. It was the beginning of an adjustment of differences, which, it is hoped, will go on till the last vestige of strife and discord shall be removed forever.

The action of the Cape May Commission was another important step in the right direction. It has not accomplished all that was hoped from it, but its influence has made for peace. It was possibly without design that in the work of that Commission, the first indispensable condition of negotiations for organic union was met. The Southern Church demanded recognition as a legitimate branch of Episcopal Methodism. This was conceded by the representatives of the Methodist Episcopal Church; and the concession places the two Churches side by side as equals, without regard to disputed points in the steps of progress towards the status of equality. It may be that our Southern brethren attach more importance to the phrase, "legitimate branch of Episcopal Methodism," than we do. Whether they do or not, will appear in the developments of the future. It does not convey to us the idea that that Church is a part of the Methodist Episcopal Church, or that its organization was authorized by any action of the General Conference of 1844. Its "legitimacy" consists in the fact that it has come to be, *de facto*, an independent Church, with all the equipments essential to an organized branch of Episcopal Methodism. There is no more occasion for doubting its legitimacy in this respect than for disputing its independence.

The Centennial Conference of Episcopal Methodism, in 1884, in the city of Baltimore, furnished an admirable proof of the possibility of thorough fellowship. The associations of that occasion will linger long in the memory of the participants. The late Ecumenical Conference, in Washington City, was cordial in brotherliness, although not particularly inspiring to hopefulness in the direction of organic union. These, together with the cheerful cordiality with which fraternal delegates are received in both General Conferences, may be taken as evidences of a mutual desire on the part of the Churches to get rid of all causes of friction, and to come to such agreements as will assure recognition and co-operation in the working field, as well as in the great ecclesiastical assemblies. This, after all, is the test of fraternity.

The progress already made toward the better understanding has not been secured without concessions. Most of these have been made by the older to the younger, by the parent body to the new branch of Episcopal Methodism which was organized in 1845. The Church has not suffered in consequence. Neither her honor nor her dignity has been impaired; and, when the time comes for other advances, the magnanimity of the Methodist Episcopal Church will be equal to all requirements for generous dealing with any branch of the Methodist family that seeks more intimate relations. She will not wait to be sought, but will seek the opportunity to encourage the consultations necessarily precedent to open negotiations for closer union. She can not afford not to hold herself ready for such consultations. The only attitude becoming her greatness is that of willingness to concede all that can be done consistently with her honor and integrity, to heal the wounds of the past, to diminish antagonisms, and restore unity, whenever unity will contribute to the enlargement of the power and the increase of the efficiency of Methodism. With her the cause for which she stands is everything. Methodism is in her thought synonymous with evangelical Christianity; and yet she has not the bigotry to claim a monopoly of either the one or the other.

The Methodist Episcopal Church, like the larger Methodism, is cosmopolitan in spirit, and can not afford to forfeit that character. She stands for the salvation of the race. Within her pale are peoples of many nationalities, complexions, and languages. These are all her children, having equal rights under her laws, and sharing equal privileges. She seeks the salvation of none whom she will not admit to her fellowship. Herein is her greatness and her strength. Her principles, which guarantee to her membership equality of rights, are fundamental. While she would gladly lead all branches of Methodism into unity, she can not lower her standard for the accommodation of any prejudices against race or color. The only ground broad enough and solid enough for her to stand upon, whether alone or in unity with other Methodisms, is the Golden Rule doctrine of equal rights in the kingdom of God. All who come into fraternity with her, or into closer union, come with full knowledge of her record, and knowing that she can not recede from the high ground taken.

Her interpretation of equality of rights is practical rather than technical. She has no sympathy with fanaticism. When the Germans, and other peoples of foreign tongues, prefer ministers and Conferences of their own, they are accommodated. When her people of color desire congregations and ministers of their own, and separate Conferences, these favors are granted. Their separation into distinct Conferences is in pursuance of their preferences, and not a disparagement. In the General Conference there is no distinction because of color or language; nor is there any distinction in the spiritual privileges of the Church, or in legal rights. It is not improbable that this breadth and catholicity will prove a serious obstacle in the way of the contemplation of organic union, although it is difficult to understand why it should be any more of a barrier in that respect than it is to formal fraternity. Hereditary biases are always peculiar, as well as stubborn. There is nothing harder to control than prejudice, perhaps because it never reasons. It was a blinding power in the disciples of our Lord while he was with them, and after his ascension. It took them nearly seven years after Pentecost to understand their duty to go to the Gentiles; and this with the world-wide commission fresh in mind as it fell from the lips of the Master, and the Holy Ghost within them as he was after the tongues of fire crowned their heads. It was not till after Peter's vision of the "great sheet," and his journey to Cæsarea, that the strange and unsuspected truth dawned upon him that "God is no respecter of persons;" nor did any of the others gain that knowledge till after Peter expounded the vision to them. But when the bonds of their Jewish prejudices were broken, and the grandeur of God's purpose of love to the nations was apprehended, they were ready to proclaim the gospel to all men of every language and complexion, and to fellowship all whose conversion they sought.

Conference fraternity is of little value if it is followed by bickerings, rivalries, crowdings, and overreachings in the actual working of the Churches in the same vicinity. It is in the congregations and homes of the people, where Christian work is done and where Christian fellowship has its purest manifestations, that genuine fraternity is to be fostered and brought to maturity. There, if anywhere, is to be laid the foundation of organic union, and there must be wrought the necessary antecedent preparation.

It is useless to talk about the union of the Churches till both people and preachers are impressed that it will be advantageous to all concerned. But the people are more easily convinced than the preachers. With them fraternity means all that the term implies. The thing needed is a profound conviction that Methodism united will be more powerful and successful than it can be in a divided condition. It seems strange that such a conviction is not universal. But there are some things to which all agree, both preachers and people, in all sections of the Church. No one doubts that Methodists ought to be fraternal. All rejoice that the bitterness engendered by obsolete controversies is dying out. All agree that if union comes it must be reached upon a basis honorable to all, and as the result of an inward persuasion which is so nearly universal as to be positively dominating. Every one will concede that the movement, in order to be either desirable or successful, must be as nearly spontaneous as is possible—the outgoing of a conviction rooted in Christian sentiment and controlling the consciousness of duty. When such a preparation comes, union will follow as naturally as ripened fruit drops to the earth.

The state of mind best calculated to hasten

this preparation, and to bring the people to right conclusions with reference to a subject so vast and many-sided, is an intense desire to know the will of God, and to do it at whatever sacrifice of preference, taste, or previously cherished opinions. The paramount aim must be to secure the approval of God; for without that, all human appliances will prove worthless in the conflict with worldliness and unbelief—a conflict whose fierceness will not diminish as the agencies of truth develop new capabilities. Methodism has always claimed to be the child of Providence; and if this claim be valid, providential indications must be accepted as authoritative, and be followed with unshrinking courage and loyalty.

God's great plans mature slowly. He is never hurried by human impatience. Why, then, should we be faithless because the preparation for reunion seems long delayed? Methodism was the first of the Churches to break her unity on the rock of slavery, and it may be that she will be the last to restore it. In her very greatness there are complications not found in smaller Churches. Let no one be discouraged because time is required. It is usually true that much more time is consumed in preparation for great events than in their achievement; and in providential plans it often happens that the larger part of the preparatory work is done without design on the part of those who do it, and by those who least intended to contribute to that end. No one expects the union of Methodism without providential agency, and no one can be certain that even his present indifference or opposition may not be used to hasten the consummation. In many ways it is true that "the wrath of man shall praise Him."

If God is in it, who shall be against it? No one can doubt that the removal of alienations between brethren, the building up of mutual confidence and love in the Church, the joining together of hearts and hands and means for the evangelization of the nations, will accord with the Divine will. Then, if God works in providential plans in harmony with his declared will, and in the direction in which his Holy Spirit, dwelling within, always draws, he does work for the union of believers in all things helpful to the Christian life and Christian activity. Those who stand in the way of such union as God approves, withstand the Spirit's drawings, and obstruct providential plans. If used as instrumentalities for enlarging the Church and giving wider scope to gospel influences, it is by that higher wisdom which overrules the selfish purposes of men to do better than they intended. Far better that we be willing workers together with God in the direct line of his graciously manifested pleasure.

IV.

IT is probably true, in all public agitations of questions in dispute, that some amusing things are to be expected—things which are not intended for amusement. Extreme partisans, in the heat of anxiety to sustain a dubious proposition, will say things seriously which, at other times, will appear to themselves, as to others, to be exceedingly ludicrous.

To those acquainted with the facts in the case, a striking illustration of this remark appears in the position taken by the representatives of the Methodist Episcopal Church, South, when they gravely asserted that slavery was not the "cause," but only the "occasion," of the division of the Church. Those not familiar with the discussions which preceded and followed the rupture of 1845 will be tempted to suppose that this could not have been more than an incidental remark, put forth in the excitement of controversy, and that by some unofficial or irresponsible disputant; but not so. It was the position deliberately chosen and formally stated by the highest officials, in sober correspondence with representatives of the Methodist Episcopal Church; so that we are compelled to disregard its ludicrous aspects, and treat it as presumably containing something important. We do it cheerfully, because it is a delight to give to those who differ from us the full benefit of their own statements.

We confess, however, to an inability to discover the special advantage accruing from this position. If we mistake not the intention of the distinction between the cause and the occasion of the division, it is to prepare the way for the allegation that the "cause" of the trouble was the agitation of the subject in the Northern States; or, in other words, that Abolitionism, and not slavery, caused the breach. The briefest answer would be that but for slavery there would have been no Abolitionism and no agitation on the subject. To unbiased minds this answer is quite sufficient. There was an unpleasant condition of things in the Conferences in the slaveholding States. The Methodist people, as well as others, had become exceedingly sensitive and restless because of the growing anti-slavery sentiment of the country, which was making itself felt in all sections, and made no promise of abatement. There is no doubt that it was hard for slaveholders to maintain loyalty to the General Conference, when it was known that the majority of that body was opposed to slavery and disposed to make effective the Disciplinary obligation to use all lawful means to extirpate the evil of that institution.

It is well known that the pro-slavery spirit was never able to brook opposition. There was disquietude, and slavery and the dread of the agitation caused it, without doubt. Slavery, by its arrogance, rendered the agitation unavoidable. Slavery was therefore both the "cause" and the "occasion" of the division. The wonder is that anybody questions it. Without slavery in the country, there would have been neither cause nor occasion for any agitation on the subject, and there is not the slightest reason to suppose that in its absence any sectional animosities could have arisen to disturb the harmony of the denomination. Slavery divided the Church, and then sought to divide the Nation, and died. Who shall mourn its departure?

Having ascertained the cause of the division, as nearly as it can be understood, it will be necessary, in reviewing the beginning and progress of the unhappy event, to consider the action of the Church prior to the division, so as to find out to what extent and in what respect the whole Church was responsible for the catastrophe. At this day it is not an assumption of superior wisdom to assert that the General Conference of 1844 made a mistake in passing the so-called "Plan of Separation." It acted in good faith and according to the best light available at the time. In order to interpret its action we must study its intention and motive. We can do this now as it could not have been done then. The light of history has come to us, dispelling both the illusions and the delusions under which the action was taken, and has revealed the pent-up passions of the friends of slavery as the judgment of charity did not at that time permit godly men to believe them possible.

There is no question as to what the General

Conference did. The record is clear. It passed an act which was subsequently called a "Plan of Separation." A complete and accurate understanding of that act is all-important. We interpret it one way, and our brethren of the South interpret it differently. In any future discussion, when we sit down together to compare notes, these different interpretations will be turned over and over again, till each shall appreciate the views of the other party.

We confess that the General Conference made a mistake; but we do not rest the cause of the old Church on that fact. What was done, was done; and, mistake as it was, we stand by the action taken. If we can not defend the course of the Church with that action standing in all the legal force that it ever acquired, it is needless to attempt its defense at all. Our Southern brethren will acknowledge the fairness of this. Then we shall be compelled to study the legal aspects of the so-called "Plan of Separation." It is not safe to assume that it became binding on the Church simply because it passed the General Conference. Its nature, intent, and its relation to the constitution of the General Conference, must all be taken into the account. All this will be done in that future, friendly discussion which we are anticipating. For the present it is enough to state the case in general terms.

The famous so-called "Plan of Separation" was not a "plan of separation" at all. It had no such purpose. There is little doubt that our Southern brethren will differ from this statement most radically. The history they have made demands it. What they assert has been heard and considered, and it is in the face of all they have said, or can say, that this position is taken. The General Conference of 1844 neither divided the Church, nor authorized its division. It made one great mistake, but it did not do the dreadful thing so often attributed to it. Its mistake consisted in making any official recognition of the probability or possibility of a subsequent division or rupture, which was threatened. It heard the intimations, and it sought to avert the calamity if possible; and if not possible, then to reduce the disaster to the minimum by marking out a way to avoid all avoidable friction. With this in view, it adopted the report of the committee, which is the famous "Plan." It was simply an outline of concessions to be made in the event the Southern Conferences should resort to the extreme act of separation. It did not induce that act, nor authorize it, nor approve it; but anticipated it, and sought to provide against avoidable evils.

There were ominous mutterings in the air. The most serious results often flow from the noblest sentiments slightly misapplied—a fact which suggests caution in accepting the action of the Church as necessarily correct when taken in times of excitement. The wisest of men, in such condition, are liable to biases which come from imperfect knowledge, dominant prejudices, or a predisposition to escape rugged issues by compromise. It is easy to discern the presence, at the time in question, of several agencies calculated to darken counsel and incline the actors to provisional adjustments which did not express the ultimate wish of either party. The action taken was a provisional compromise, conditioned on events predicted on one side as liable to come to pass unless some such action were taken, and which all deplored and pledged themselves to avert if possible. The motives of those who yielded to the pressure put upon them by the persistent predictions of disaster in the form of division or secession, have not been called in question. They deplored the rupture only less than the surrender of principle in relation to the chief and only cause of the disquietude. If they felt the breath of the gathering storm, and quailed as they looked upon its angry brow, they stood boldly for the right in principle, while they went to the verge of the allowable in their efforts to conciliate the disaffected. It is no disparagement of their wisdom or loyalty to hold that the results of their concessions prove to us that a higher wisdom would have refused compromise, and thrown the whole responsibility upon the dissatisfied. The rupture could not have come more certainly, and would not have been more violent, while the necessity of bearing the responsibility, without any shadow of authorization, might have sobered the judgment and moderated the passions of those who marched at the head of the outgoing procession.

Conceding the mistake of the General Conference in passing the report which has been construed as authorizing the division of the Church, it is important to consider to what extent that action bound the Church, and whether the conditions underlying it were so met as to give it legal force in the actual disruption. We shall see that the conditions were not met, and that it never was lawfully carried into effect; but, for the present, it is confessed that there was in it the appearance of authority for division enough to impress those unacquainted with its history, and unfamiliar with the peculiarities of the constitution of the General Conference and the limitations of its power, with the idea that the subsequent proceedings of the Southern Conferences were in pursuance of authority given them by the General Conference. The real issue with the Southern Church is at this point. That Church holds that the apparent authorization was real; that the "Plan" was legal, and became effective; that the whole Church was bound by it; and that, consequently, the division was legitimate, and not a secession. In confirmation of this claim, appeal is made to the decision of the United States

Court, which held that the Southern Church was entitled to its share of the property of the Book Concern. We concede that the court decision was favorable to that Church, and that, so far as it touched the legality of the "Plan," it sustained it. In all this there is nothing to contravene the view expressed with reference to the conditionality of the so-called "Plan," and its failure to become binding as an act of the Church. The decision of the court was reached after the consummation of the division, and largely on the ground of equity, which was scarcely disputed. The court itself, as is well known, was in strong sympathy with Southern sentiments on the slavery issue; so that it is not hard to show that the legal decision never represented the meaning of the General Conference. Beyond the legal issue before it, the dictum of the court was extra-judicial, and of no force as an interpretation of the action of the General Conference. The Church promptly accepted the decision of the court, and acknowledged its substantial justice in relation to the property question; but the people who knew the facts were far from accepting its dictum as decisive with reference to the binding character of the so-called "Plan of Separation." The delegates in the General Conference, who were actors in the construction and adoption of that document, were quite as competent as any civil tribunal to determine whether or not it was a completed action; and they could not, if they would, at the behest of any popular clamor, sink their own intelligence in the presence of any extra-judicial declaration. They well knew that, while all the facts and considerations which controlled the General Conference were not in the record and could not be made tangible to the court, there were material conditions understood by the delegates, which secured the adoption of the "Plan," and which were so utterly disregarded after its adoption that not even the semblance of an effort to comply with them could be alleged.

The majority of the delegates supposed they had reason to believe that their fellow-delegates from the Southern Conferences were as anxious to avoid disruption as themselves. Throughout the debate, all references to it as a possibility had been made in the language of deprecation.

It was treated as a prospective calamity, rather than as a desired outcome of strained relations. There was, therefore, a general expectation that the Southern delegates would return to their homes and Conferences with the loyalty they professed, and use their influence to allay the excitement that was supposed to exist, and do all they could to induce the Conferences to continue their allegiance to the Church. This was understood to be pledged in connection with the adoption of the "Plan," which has figured so largely as a "Plan of Separation;" and there is scarcely the shadow of a probability that it could have been adopted without such pledge, expressed or implied. But the Southern delegates did nothing of the kind. They began at once the preparation for calling a convention to consider the situation, looking to the separation. It was supposed from the debates that the trouble was with the people, who would be unwilling to receive pastors sent to them from Conferences under the jurisdiction of the General Conference so strongly committed to anti-slavery sentiments. This provisional "Plan" was to be used as proof of the liberal disposition of the Church, and of its willingness to conciliate the dissatisfied, as far as possible, without the sacrifice of principle. Advantage was at once taken of this effort at conciliation, and the claim set up that division was authorized and sanctioned. Instead of the people rising in opposition to the authority of the Conferences, the preachers themselves moved for separation without consulting the people. All this, and more, will be seen in that future interchange of thought which we are anticipating; but there are two or three other points that must be indicated in this preparatory outline of the situation.

V.

IF our Southern brethren desire to keep the distinction between the "cause" and the "occasion" of the disruption before their minds, and wish to be strictly accurate in its statement, they will recognize the fact that slavery was the "cause," and that the action of the General Conference in the case of Bishop Andrew was the "occasion," of that sad event.

Prior to the General Conference of 1844, Bishop James O. Andrew married a widow who was the owner of a number of slaves. In this way he came to be a slaveholder in the eye of the law and of public sentiment. This relation to the institution was offensive to the great body of the Church over which he was a general superintendent. It was also plainly in violation of the law of the Church as it had been interpreted from the beginning. There was no possibility that the General Conference could pass without some expression of disapproval. Early in the session the attention of the body was called to the subject. Several lines of action were proposed, but the General Conference was not inclined to extreme measures. It finally passed a resolution declaring its judgment that it would be expedient for Bishop Andrew to desist from the exercise of episcopal functions till he could free himself from his objectionable relation to slavery. He was not tried, nor deposed, nor suspended. It was only by implication that he could be considered censured. Considering the gravity of the case, and the sensitiveness of the Church in large sections of the country, the action was extremely mild. There were Annual Conferences, equal in rights and dignity to any in the connection, that would not transact business with a slaveholding bishop presiding over them. His relation to the institution was therefore an impediment to the performance of his duties. In reason he could expect nothing less than the action that was taken. But this very mild action was offensive to the South, and was made the pretext for further agitation. It was construed as a suspension without formal trial, and denounced as arbitrary and unlawful. There is no doubt that the impression prevails widely in the Southern States till this day that the General Conference of 1844 dealt harshly with Bishop Andrew, transcending its legitimate power in order to humiliate him because of an innocent connection with a time-honored institution. The people have been so taught, and will so believe till the exact truth is brought to them, which can be done only through channels hitherto not open for this purpose.

The Southern delegates who participated in the adoption of the so-called "Plan," so far as was ever ascertained, made no effort to allay the excitement and maintain the unity of the Church. Their course would scarcely have been different if division had been a foregone conclusion, deliberately preferred, and simply awaiting a plausible excuse. The excuse or "occasion" came in the case of Bishop Andrew, and measures were set on foot that were never contemplated in the "Plan." The Louisville Convention was called to meet in 1845. That Convention was unauthorized by any action of the General Conference, unprovided for in the "Plan," and was without power to represent the Methodist Episcopal Church, or to do anything in her name, or to take any action that would in any sense be binding upon her as a denomination. It was purely a Southern affair, the creature of Southern Annual Conferences, with delegates from no other section of the Church. No effort had been made to reconcile the disaffected in those Conferences to the action of the General Conference; nor had time been allowed in which to cool the passions that had been aroused, or to test the question as to whether the Churches would submit to be served by pastors sent from Conferences in allegiance to the General Conference. This unauthorized Louisville Convention was called instead, as if for the express purpose of thwarting the plans of the General Conference. The real nature of the division can not be comprehended without this consideration of the utterly unofficial and unauthorized character of this Convention, and its absolute want of power in its relation to the Methodist Episcopal Church.

To all this must be added another statement with regard to that famous "Plan," which is as vital as anything yet suggested. It is that, whatever obligations this "Plan" might have imposed on the Church to follow its provisions for adjusting affairs after the Southern Conferences had decided to leave its jurisdiction, that obligation could not be complete or binding till the provisions of the "Plan" itself, for rendering the proposed settlement lawful, were carried out. To render that settlement lawful, according to the "Plan," required compliance with the provision for changing the constitution of the General Conference. The General Conference proposed, in the contingency now understood, to do certain things which the constitution expressly prohibited it from doing; and therefore the change of the constitution, or the suspension of its limitation, was indispensable. Some of the stipulations in the "Plan" expressly required the suspension of the Restrictive Rule by the constitutional process; and in the absence of that suspension, which was never effected, and for which the Southern Conferences did not wait, there was no possibility of legalizing proceedings under the "Plan." It seems to some of us that our brethren in the Southern Church have not appreciated this point; but, in that brotherly discussion which is coming, they will look it in the face as never before, and give us credit for regarding the organic law of the General Conference as superior to a tentative report adopted by that body. It will be said, in this connection, that the force of this position is not so great, since the particular part of the "Plan," which was in terms submitted to the process for suspending the Restrictive Rule, related to the division of the Book Concern property, and not to the fixing of the geographical line. There are two answers to this. The first is, that the "Plan" was a unit, and the failure of one essential part of it to become legal involved the failure of the whole. The suspension of the Restrictive Rule was a fundamental condition of the contract, which contract could be nothing more than tentative while the suspension was pending, whatever might be done on the other side. The Louisville Convention met, and divided the Church as far as it could—that is, it declared the Southern Conferences a separate and independent Church—before the Restrictive Rule could be suspended, and, therefore, before the "Plan" could be legalized under the law of the Church.

Another answer is, that whatever the fate of the provision for suspending the Restrictive Rule on the property question, the act of the General Conference, looking to a voluntary relinquishment of its jurisdiction over any part or section of the Church, was necessarily null and void, it being an act in violation of the constitution under which it exists and exercises its functions. The General Conference is a delegated body of limited power, acting as agent for constituent bodies, empowered to "make rules and regulations for the Church," but not to relegate or turn over any Annual Conference, or any fraction of the Church, however small, to the jurisdiction or government of any other body. This principle is fundamental.

The constitutional limitations of the General Conference have been studied more carefully since that action was taken than before. Other occasions have arisen to call attention to them. It has been decided that the body has no power to alter its composition, except by what is known as the Restrictive Rule process. It could not admit a layman as a delegate without that process; and, at the session of 1888, it was decided, after full discussion, that it could not admit women under the general provision for lay representation. How, then, could it authorize a division of the Church, and turn over half of its constituency to the jurisdiction of an entirely different body yet to be formed? The thing is preposterous on its face. If we should admit that the General Conference did not take this view of its limitations, but really supposed itself competent to authorize the Southern Conferences to form a new General Conference, that does not alter the fact. Its ignorance of the law could not enhance its power, or render legal that which was illegal when the law is understood. It did not intend to override the constitution. It expressly provided that the Restrictive Rule process should be observed with regard to essential parts of the "Plan;" and as the "Plan" was a unit, the failure of an essential part would be the failure of the whole. Nor was there any deception or improper dealing in this. The "party of the other part" was present, understanding all that was done, taking part in the proceedings, and having knowledge of the contingencies depending on the action of the Annual Conferences. The whole story is told when it is said that the General Conference ventured beyond the border of its legitimate power in the interest of peace; but it neither divided the Church, nor authorized its division. If it had expressly provided that the Southern Conferences should leave its jurisdiction and set up for themselves, its action would have been null and void, being in violation of its constitution.

Just here some one will ask, "Why this presentation of the legal aspects of the division, in connection with the question of reunion?" The answer is, we must understand the position that each has taken in the past, in order to appreciate the grounds occupied at the present. So long as our Southern brethren believe we made a law and then disregarded it, they will cherish towards us feelings quite obstructive of intelligent negotiations. Their people have never gotten a just understanding of our view of the legal ground on which we have stood all these years. They have regarded our position as that of truce-breakers, and their own as law-abiding. A full knowledge of the facts would disabuse their minds. It would astonish them greatly, no doubt, but it would promote mutual respect, and facilitate approaches towards the better condition so ardently desired.

It is not doubted that the Convention which determined the existence of the Methodist Episcopal Church, South, kept the so-called "Plan of Separation" in view, and sought to conform to its outline of arrangement for the new Church. We may concede that it treated the "Plan" as a lawful thing; that it accepted it as a charter, and looked to it as legally authorizing its proceedings, and as the basis of its claim for a division of the property and funds of the Church. It may have entertained this belief, and acted upon it; but its ignorance of the defect in its legality did not remedy the defect. No matter what the members of that Convention thought, the fact is both plain and stubborn that the "Plan" was never legally enacted under the constitution of the General Conference, and never could have been, even with the concurrence of the three-fourths of the members of the Annual Conferences. Such a vote could lift the restrictions on the power of the General Conference to make rules and regulations "for the Church," but it could never empower it to legislate against the Church, or to divide or destroy the Church. The conclusion is therefore inevitable that, legally speaking, there is no authority in or for the Methodist Episcopal Church, South, as a legitimate branch of Episcopal Methodism older or greater than the Louisville Convention. If antecedent Annual Conference action constituted the Convention, the Convention constituted the Church. In that Convention the Methodist Episcopal Church, as a Church, was not represented; and there is no sense in which it could be bound by the action of that Convention. Hence the further conclusion is inevitable, however distasteful to those who have never admitted it, that the act of the Louisville Convention in establishing a separate and independent Church, was nothing other than an act of secession.

Notwithstanding the haste and unlawfulness of the proceedings culminating in that unauthorized Convention, the Methodist Episcopal Church was still disposed to settle all questions at issue according to the "Plan." It was in the act of taking the vote in the Annual Conferences on the suspension of the Restrictive Rule, as the "Plan" provided, in order to legalize as far as possible the division of the property, when the Southern Church interrupted the proceeding, and nullified all obligation in that direction, by resorting to the secular court to enforce its claim—a claim the mother Church was providing to grant as rapidly as was possible under the constitution and under the terms of the "Plan." This turn of affairs, notwithstanding the court gave the new Church its claim, destroyed the vitality of the "Plan," if it ever had any vitality, and gave to the new organization the full character of a secession from the Methodist Episcopal Church.

The story is a sad one. Its full rehearsal will reveal mistakes on both sides. The excess of passion was with those who hastened to go out from a jurisdiction which was odious to them because it antagonized slavery and refused to tolerate slaveholding in the episcopacy. Passion begets passion. The strong men of Methodism wept at witnessing their beloved Church torn in sunder by the foul spirit of slavery, and their righteous indignation flamed forth in words that burned. Strong language was inevitable. While slavery lived, the breach was irreparable. It came as a calamity, and it is a calamity still. Must the effect continue, now that the cause is removed? or is there wisdom and piety enough in Methodism to grapple successfully with the problem of restoration? Shall the present generation solve the problem, or shall it be transmitted to the generation following?

Some of us believe the time is here for beginning the solution. The great public outside of Methodism believes it ought to be done. It will not be an easy matter to meet our obligations to the Christian sentiment of the country if we withstand the influences at work in society tending to bury the old enmities, and to bring into the Church and business and social life of the Nation that community of interest and feeling which is so becoming and so essential to the country's welfare. There are claims upon us as a Christian people that should be deemed not less binding than our obligation to obey our peculiar tastes and preferences in ecclesiastical affairs. If our devotion to antiquated social prejudices prove detrimental to Christian faith in general, the duty is imperative to conquer them, even though we might individually serve God and get to heaven without abandoning our narrowness.

VI.

THE supposed geographical line between the two Churches, and its observance, must have its share of attention. At one time it was thought to be an important part of the contract between the parties, if the word contract can be admitted with reference to the then existing conditions. It was perhaps as binding as any other part of the famous "Plan."

That "Plan," which was from its inception unconstitutional, tentative, conditional, and never legalized, contained a provision for dividing the territory of the country, so that the jurisdiction of the new Church, if one should be formed, would be confined to such Annual Conferences in the slaveholding States as would prefer to leave the jurisdiction of the Methodist Episcopal Church. According to the wording of the "Plan," it is evident that the line was to be a fixed boundary, over which neither Church was to pass. As the whole was intended to operate in the interest of peace, this dividing line was regarded as indispensable. No one disputes that the General Conference of 1844 adopted the report of a committee which described the line, and made it as binding as any other part of the "Plan." If the other provisions of that report had been concurred in by the Annual Conferences, as was contemplated, and if the Southern Church had abode by the whole "Plan" till the final action was taken, the Church whose General Conference perpetrated the blunder of making such an agreement would have observed it with scrupulous fidelity.

The Convention of the Southern Conferences, which met in Louisville, Ky., in 1845, and declared independence and separation from the Methodist Episcopal Church, adopted the same line, and bound the new Church by its action as completely as by any other action taken by it. The Convention, acting originally in the premises, unfettered by the constitutional limitations which bound the General Conference of the previous year, was at liberty to establish the line described in the General Conference action, or any other that its judgment might dictate, as the limit of the jurisdiction of the new Church. It saw fit to adopt the line as described in the so-called "Plan," with an additional provision or construction that changed it from a fixed to a movable line. That is, it provided that a vote should be taken in the congregations bordering on the line as to whether they would adhere to the old Church or go with the new one; and when a congregation on the south side of the line should adhere to the old Church, the next charge south would become the border, and be entitled to make its choice by vote. Its thought was, no doubt, to push the line northward, as it confidently expected some of the river towns and cities in Ohio and Indiana to vote to go into the Southern Church.

It is not exactly clear as to how it expected the vote to be taken on the north side of the Ohio River, unless it anticipated that some of the preachers and congregations would be so strongly inclined to adhere South that they would voluntarily proceed to vote without waiting any Conference action or order; for it is hardly supposable that the members of that

Convention could expect the Methodist Episcopal Church to feel bound to carry out the arrangements of the Convention with reference to the vote. It is scarcely possible to believe that the intelligent members of the Convention were not fully apprised, at the time, that the Church had come to regard the act of the General Conference as a blunder, and to see that it was unconstitutional, and could never become law, even in the sense contemplated by the formal suspension of the Restrictive Rule. Whether they knew it or not, it is true that many of the delegates had declared that they voted for the "Plan" under a misapprehension; that they did not anticipate the immediate calling of a Convention to effect a division of the Church; that such a movement was contrary to the general understanding, and that it vitiated the essential terms of the compact, implied or expressed in the action taken.

It follows from the foregoing considerations that the line finally drawn had no greater authority behind it than the Louisville Convention; that it was binding only on the Southern Church; that the movable feature in connection with it was impracticable for good, and liable to be a source of irritation and friction; and, finally, that it defeated its own purpose by opening the way for both Churches to occupy the same territory. This last suggestion is worthy of more attention than it has received.

There has been much complaint against the Methodist Episcopal Church for entering Kentucky and other Border States, and organizing Churches on territory claimed by the Southern Church. We do not pretend that our only right to enter that territory is found in the provision of the Louisville Convention, in connection with the movable feature of the line; but it is certain that that provision was itself ample to justify the old Church in continuing to minister to those who preferred her ministry on that side of the line. In other words, the Southern Church made provision for the old Church to re-establish herself on the south side of the line in all places where the congregations voted against adhering to the new Church.

The writer has distinct recollections on this subject. In 1845, shortly after the close of the Louisville Convention, the preachers sent by the Kentucky Conference to charges on the Ohio River, began to take the vote in the congregations on the question as to whether they would adhere North or South, as they expressed it. A goodly number of congregations in Kentucky voted to remain in the old Church. These were at once abandoned by their Southern pastors, and left at liberty to receive preachers sent to them from the other side of the river. The Rev. John Meek, at that time traveling the Georgetown Circuit in the old Ohio Conference, was sent over to gather up these abandoned congregations, and reorganize the Methodist Episcopal Church in Kentucky; and the writer was employed to fill the place vacated by him when he went to perform that duty. The several congregations in that State which voted against entering the Southern Church never lost their standing as members of the Methodist Episcopal Church; and consequently the old Church never lost her footing in that State, and is not there as an intruder or a newcomer into territory previously occupied by another Church. She represents the original Methodism of Kentucky; her line of succession there is unbroken; and she is there by prescriptive right under the action of the Louisville Convention, as well as by the original right which she never lawfully forfeited.

The next point worthy of consideration in this connection is, that after fixing the line that was supposed to restrict their labors to the slaveholding States, our Southern brethren did not keep themselves to their own side of the line. They crossed it, not to minister to congregations abandoned by the old Church—on voting to join the Southern Church—but to break into existing congregations which had not voted, and were not required to vote, on the subject. They came into Cincinnati, where they found sympathy and friends, and established two congregations. The efforts of Rev. Dr. Sehon, Rev. Dr. Latta, Rev. Wm. Burke, Rev. G. W. Maley, and others, to establish Southern Methodism in Cincinnati, are not yet forgotten. The history of "Soule Chapel," and of the Southern occupancy of Union Chapel, when written up, will make a strange chapter in the records of Cincinnati Methodism. It will show that the Southern Church, a'ter making the line, first disregarded it, and made desperate efforts to hold permanently ground temporarily gained in the free State of Ohio.

This early effort in Cincinnati was not the last made by the Southern Church to push beyond her self-prescribed boundaries. She asserts her right to go where she will as positively as does the old Church. There is little heard about her movements to plant herself on what was never slave territory; and possibly this is accounted for by the fact that no one objects to her coming, or persecutes her ministers for coming. Some people will be astonished to learn that she has gone outside of the limits originally imposed upon herself. The facts are not widely known.

While the war was in progress there were some noted politicians in Ohio who violently opposed its prosecution, and kept themselves in full sympathy with the South. Among them was the once famous Edson B. Olds, an ex-congressman, of Lancaster, Ohio. He had been a Methodist, and retained a nominal connection with the Church, but was intensely embittered towards everything that sustained the Government in its efforts to subdue rebellion. He determined to leave the Church, and to have one organized that should be after his own heart politically, and free from all suspicion of loyalty to the Government. He issued a call for a public meeting in the court-house, in Lancaster, to take steps towards the organization of such a Church. The court-house bell rang at the hour appointed for the meeting; the crowd from the streets, the hotels, and the saloons, came together—the young hoodlums of the place in the majority. Mr. Olds called the meeting to order, and nominated 'Squire Reese as chairman, and Virgil E. Shaw as secretary. These were elected by the vote of the crowd, many of the boys voting both ways. The chairman could not state the object of the meeting, and called on Mr. Olds to perform that duty. Mr. Olds did so in a long speech, in which he berated the Churches and the Government in a lively manner. After his speech, the secretary presented a paper setting forth the abominations of the Churches, and the necessity of a new organization. This was followed by resolutions, previously prepared, declaring the

Church organized, and inviting a minister of an adjoining county, of notorious disloyalty, to become pastor. The paper and resolutions were adopted by the vote of the same motley crowd, many voting again on both sides. The meeting then adjourned. No attempt was made to have religious services. The new Church thus born was called the "Christian Union." Disaffected members of the different Churches subsequently went into it, all on political grounds. It spread through sections of Indiana and Illinois. The Rev. Mr. Ditzler, of the Methodist Episcopal Church, South, came into Southern Illinois, and found it there. He became interested in it, and finally induced it, or a section of it, to change its name, and be called the Episcopal Methodist Church. This was the name the Southern Church was trying to take at that time, but failed because the necessary vote in the Annual Conferences could not be secured. Under this name this peculiar organization was recognized by the Southern General Conference. It was represented in that body, and, finally, after the failure to change the name of the Southern Methodist Church, this same Episcopal Methodist Church became the present Illinois Conference of the Methodist Episcopal Church, South. It is in full communion with that Church, and the bishops make their annual visits to it, and preside over it the same as other Conferences. The Methodist Episcopal Church never abuses them for coming, and never objects to any good they do, or to any expenses they incur in trying to support this feeble, uninfluential Conference in our midst.

It is more generally known that the Methodist Episcopal Church, South, has pushed its way into Colorado, California, Oregon, and Montana. Its position in some of these States is not very enviable; but the old Church makes no war on any of the people who prefer that communion. There is no doubt that our Southern brethren have reasons satisfactory to themselves for going to the trouble and expense of organizing and trying to sustain their Church in these distant States. To us their presence there seems useless and distracting; yet that is their business, not ours.

After the war and the emancipation of the slaves, the Southern States were greatly impoverished, and Southern Methodism shared in the general depression. Her resources were greatly reduced, and of necessity she was heavily taxed to supply the means of grace to the needy poor within her chosen borders; yet in her poverty she did not husband all her means to meet the demands at home, but pushed her agencies into regions beyond. As shown above, she went to California and Oregon; she planted her banners in Colorado and Montana, and, looking longingly into the broad prairies of Illinois, she joined herself to the "Christian Union" faction of political malcontents, and took them to her bosom and fellowship, and still bears the burden, which is not a light one.

It is easy to see why the old Church should go South to meet needs that were not met; but to disinterested on-lookers it is not possible to discover any good reason why the Southern Church should expend so much of her limited means in crowding into the Northwest, to build herself up through the political prejudices of people out of sympathy with their surroundings. It is hard, indeed, to resist the impression that her chief mission in the North and in the West is to minister to political animosities, and encourage prejudices that ought never to have been born.

In the general depression which followed the war, the Methodist Episcopal Church, which really never knew geographical limitations, went into the Southern States to build churches, to plant schools, and to preach the gospel to the needy. She went on a mission of peace and good-will; she extended the helping hand to all classes, without regard to previous conditions or relations or political biases. She went to bless the people, by ministering to urgent needs and lifting communities into a better life. Her work was intended to be conciliatory and evangelistic, and it should have been met in the spirit of brotherliness. It was a mistake that Southern Methodism did not hail her coming with delight. In many respects the work of the Methodist Episcopal Church in the Southern States since the war has been as heroic and philanthropic as any in her history.

It is not claimed that no mistakes have been made in her progress. She has not always been fortunate in her representatives, and therefore not always wise or discreet in her methods.

It was inevitable that some should reach the front and assume prominence whose records had not been the brightest, and whose qualifications for leadership were not of the highest order. This imposed double burdens on the noble men who went out with honorable rank and unsullied name, at great sacrifice of comfort and position, to do the Lord's work for the sake of the Lord and his poor. Such were worthy of double honor, and their memories will ever be held in highest esteem. They have done work in which the angels delight, and some of them have gone to the reward of the righteous.

Some mistakes have been made in method and policy, as well as in judgment with regard to locations. Failures have followed, of course, as they were inevitable under the circumstances; but, bating failures caused by mistakes, the success of the work inaugurated among the poorer classes—white as well as black—has been such as to justify the expenditures made as a whole. Unfortunately, some of the failures which have occurred have been in the more prominent places, and, although clearly exceptional, can be pointed to as conspicuous examples of large outlays for insignificant returns, and thus be used to impress the public unfavorably. The study of these exceptional cases has caused some good people to conclude that the work of the Methodist Episcopal Church among the white people of the Southern States is a mistake. But this reasoning from particular cases to general conclusions is neither logical nor safe. The study of all the facts, including the preferences and needs of the people reached and benefited, gives a wider view, and one that yields much greater satisfaction.

Whether the work in question has been successful or not, it has been prosecuted under difficulties formidable enough to discourage any but the most heroic; while the principles underlying our occupancy of that field are too sacred to be surrendered, and our motives too pure to permit regrets.

VII.

SINCE the great revival in the Churches of this country in 1857, there has been a marked tendency on the part of ecclesiastical bodies of similar faith to consolidate for Christian work. The distractions of the war period did not destroy this tendency, but rather increased it. The influence of the "Christian Commission," organized for the purpose of alleviating the distresses of the war, was highly beneficial in the way of securing the co-operation of the Churches. The Old and New School Presbyterian bodies came together as by a common inspiration. The Methodist bodies in Canada rejoice in the new strength brought to them by the oneness achieved. The sorest rending of all—that which was on the slavery issue—is in the course of healing in the other Churches, and there is no good reason why it should not be with the Methodists. At least that is the conviction of many; and so widely does this opinion prevail, in and out of Methodist circles, that it devolves upon those who oppose the healing to furnish the reasons for continued separation. The object of this treatise is to impress this thought, so that the responsibility shall rest where it properly belongs, in the event of further rivalries and antagonisms.

With some the claim is set up that there can be no discussion of the subject of organic union so long as we continue to occupy the territory claimed by the Southern Church in the Southern States. We are called upon to withdraw our ministers, schools, colleges, and all our forces, from the South, as a condition precedent to any consideration of the future relations of the Churches. It might be a proper retort to reply that we can not think of this withdrawal till the Southern Church withdraws from the soil which has never felt the blighting touch of slavery. But mere retort is not argument. As we have never objected to their coming, we shall not ask them to withdraw. It is not improbable that they reach a class of people in the Northern States whose prejudices are too great to allow them to be benefited by our ministry so long as there is a ministry of the Southern type at hand.

It is not clear that the joint occupancy of the same territory is inimical to future union. It may be; but who can tell? Above the intentions of the actors there is possibly a providential purpose in this overlapping of the two Methodisms. In its first results there is friction, of necessity, and a severe test of the fraternal spirit. Why may not this be the means of showing us the folly and waste of division? It often happens that the things which look like obstacles turn to the furtherance of the gospel. The collisions of this joint occupancy at once beget oppositions, and suggest consolidation as the remedy. It will not be astonishing if the first real demand for union shall come from fields where the conflict is the sharpest. Those who feel the burden of the rivalry, will also feel the need of the better condition, and will open their hearts widest to welcome the advent of peace and good-will; just as the soldiers that stood bravest in the brunt of battle were the most cordial in the fraternity that came after the war.

The arguments in favor of a united Methodism are too palpable to need formal statement. Union is better than division, if it can possibly be had; and whatever men may think of the expediency of looking and praying for it when the prospect of accomplishing it is so remote, the hopeful anticipation of it is not disloyalty to Christ. When the question is fairly open, and the mountains of difficulty that now stand forbiddingly in the way shall be seen in their proper dimensions as hills of moderate elevation, but little courage will be required to enter the lists, and contend for that which the noblest Christian sentiment gladly accepts as the will of God. What is in demand at the present time is a faith broad and vigorous enough to look beyond the environments of the hour, and take hold of the possibilities of the future, when the spirit of consecration shall lift the millions of American Methodists into the light and freedom of unselfish love to God and willing co-operation with providential plans. In such a future, who can imagine reasons to justify continued divisions?

It is not difficult to draw pleasant pictures

of the millennial state of the Church, when the nations shall yield to the peaceful sway of our holy Christianity, and when the spiritual brotherhood of the followers of Christ shall become a veritable realization; but to bring about that happy condition, or to do the best thing towards hastening it, is quite a different task. The man who dreams of the coming glory of the Church does no harm, and by painting his visions for others he may stimulate faith and hope, and be useful; but he who takes the Church and the world as he finds them, and uses all the power of a devoted life in lifting burdens from others, and removing stumbling-blocks from the pathway of anxious souls, does more to help the Church forward to the brighter day than is possible to any dreamer of beautiful dreams.

It is not possible to stimulate zeal for the reunion of Methodism till the persuasion of its practicability becomes prevalent, to quite a considerable extent, in the several branches of the Church to be affected. Fancy pictures of the advantages of union will be of little service so long as there is no hope of making them realities. Every turn of the subject brings us back to the question of possibility. In studying this question, in order to be perfectly fair, we must assume the moral preparation for it; that is, we must proceed on the supposition that all parties are ready and willing for it, provided it can be brought about without any humiliations, and without sacrifices too great to be considered. We do not mean to say that this moral preparation exists now as a matter of fact, although it is highly probable that there is more of it in the Churches than is largely suspected; but the thought is, that in looking at the possibility of the adjustment of questions of business and office and government, we are to regard all parties as favorably disposed, so that nothing shall stand in the way but those things which are real and tangible. Every one can see that parties willing to come to an honorable agreement can conquer difficulties that would be unconquerable to the unwilling. So it is in looking at the question of possibility as an abstract question. If one is indisposed to the union, his mind will magnify the difficulties in the way till what will seem practicable to others, will appear to him absolutely impossible. It therefore follows that some moral preparation is necessary to the unbiased study of the abstract question of the possibility of ultimate Methodist union. He only is qualified to look at it impartially who is willing to be convinced upon reasonable grounds. All that is asked in this direction is freedom from positive prejudice.

The question of officers will come into the account, whether we desire it or not. One of the economies of union is in the matter of official positions. Fewer officers in the general work of the Church will be required with the consolidation than with the division, as at present. It can not be believed, however, that the reduction of offices to be filled can become a serious question in its relation to the possibility of union, whatever influence it may have in determining the desirability of this consummation. Fewer bishops will be necessary with one Church than with two; but all the bishops in office will not be too many when the union is effected, only the necessity for the election of others will not be so great; so that the union will only interfere with the prospects of a few persons who may anticipate this promotion. Such an outcome is unavoidable; but who can see in this anything bearing on the question of the practicability of the reunion? The same is true of the other offices, only the reduction will not be so great as might be supposed. About as many publishing agents will be required for the Book Concerns, and probably the same number of editors for official papers. The aggregate number of missionary secretaries, and secretaries for other Church boards, would probably not be so great as now; but who can see anything in this that has to do with this question of possibility? The whole matter of offices and officers could be settled without friction by intelligent negotiations.

The great question relates to the government of so large a body as would be our united Methodism. The trouble is not in having so many people amenable to the same Discipline—for the laws that govern a million are equally adapted to the government of any number of millions—but the representation of the larger number in the General Conference is a question of serious import. Already the General Conference is large. Many think it too large for convenience or successful work. That some improvement in its methods to secure greater deliberation is important, is beyond question. The near future must bring some radical changes in the ratio of representation, and it is not impossible to devise such regulations as will secure equal rights to ten millions as well as to five or three. It is only necessary to recognize the unquestionable fact that two competent delegates can represent a Conference, for all the purposes of wise legislation, as well as five. Whether the reunion comes or not, the time is coming when the largest Conferences in the connection will be satisfied with less than half the delegates they now send. Two ministers can represent the largest Conference as well as two laymen.

In the consolidation the number of the Annual Conferences will not be increased to the extent that the first thought would suggest. In the territory where there is now overlapping, there would be consolidations that would prevent the increase of the number of the Conferences. A goodly number of Conferences in both Churches would be absorbed and cease to be Conferences.

The Southern Conferences in Illinois, Colorado, California, Oregon, and Montana would be absorbed in other Conferences on the same ground. Such would be the fate of our smaller Conferences in Virginia, North Carolina, Georgia, and in all the Southern States. Besides these, there are other consolidations possible; so that in the reorganization of the work, while there would be an increase of large Conferences, there would be such a reduction in the number of small Conferences that, in the aggregate, the number of Annual Conferences represented in the General Conference would not be much greater than at the present time. A careful computation will show that a General Conference of six hundred delegates will amply represent the consolidated Methodism of the entire country.

It is conceded that a body of that size is somewhat inconvenient. As to the matter of entertainment, there is no trouble to be apprehended. Delegates will not be quartered on private hospitality as in former years at any rate. The whole Church will bear the expense, which will be lighter in proportion than at the present. The rules of order and of business can be arranged so that confusion and delay and loss of time can be avoided, making the larger body as deliberate and efficient, and even more methodical than our General Conferences have been for several sessions past. It is therefore needless to be deterred from the consideration of so great an achievement on the ground that our legislative and governmental machinery can not be adapted to so great a constituency. The regular growth of the Church as it is requires frequent modifications of the ratio of representation, and all that is necessary is willingness to come to a basis that will admit of an indefinite increase of membership and ministers, without enlarging the General Conference to absolutely unwieldy proportions. This will probably be reached in time by adopting a plan of Conference representation, modeled more after the United States Senate than the House of Representatives. When the minimum number of ministers necessary to the existence of an Annual Conference shall be considerably raised, and when no Conference, however large, shall be entitled to more than two ministerial delegates, and the smaller ones to one each, a basis will be fixed that will be permanent. Then will the possibility of combinations for election purposes be almost, if not entirely, destroyed; and then also will an election to the General Conference be an honor indeed, as it will be the expression of the judgment of the majority freely given. In such conditions the fittest men will be chosen. Accommodation and complimentary elections will go out of fashion. Character and experience will count for more than the less solid qualities which often secure popularity and prominence, while adroitness in management will be at a discount.

It is said, as an embarrassment in the way of reunion, that the Churches have diverged so much in "rules and regulations" that any coming together will be impossible. This is an imaginary trouble. In a few things there has been divergence; but not in anything that relates to doctrines or morals, or in anywise involves conscience. There are differences with respect to the order of District Conferences, the method of electing lay delegates, and some other matters of that sort. Possibly the most serious is, that the Southern Church has abolished the plan of receiving members on probation. We retain the old practice of making the minimum term of probation six months, and will not be likely to surrender the principle. The condition of the work has changed since the period of six months was made the shortest term, so that the purposes of probation can be as well met in half the time. In former years the large circuit system kept the preachers from the opportunity of speedy acquaintance with the applicants for membership; but now the majority of converts come through the Sabbath-school, and all are so immediately under the watch-care of the pastor that three months will give him a better knowledge of his people, and better opportunity to learn the character of candidates for membership, than six months did in the early years of Methodism. In special cases, where three months are not sufficient, the term could be prolonged to six or nine months, or indefinitely, when necessary. The three months' probation would answer every purpose as the minimum; and there is little doubt that the Southern Church, after its experience without any probation, would find it advantageous to retrace its steps to this extent. When once the spirit of union possesses the two bodies, all these differences of regulation can be harmonized without trouble or sacrifice. In fact, the question of the possibility of the consolidation turns not on any of these matters, but solely on the moral preparation for it. If the Churches are not willing for it, but deliberately prefer separation, that settles the question, and banishes all hope, till superabounding grace brings more light and a better spirit.

VIII.

TO some it will occur that, up to this point, the most serious feature of this whole business has been passed over without mention. The subject of color has been alluded to more than once, yet only in a general way. The principle that guides the Methodist Episcopal Church has been clearly presented. In all that relates to legal rights or spiritual privileges in the Church of God, she knows no difference in race, language, color, or nationality. All who are converted at her altars are welcomed to her communion.

It is a matter of regret that there is any question of color to be considered in connection with the future relations of Methodists, or any any other Christian people; but the question is here, and it will have its place in this general subject in spite of our wishes to the contrary. If we could but follow the law of the gospel, as indicated above, and know nothing of distinctive races or colors in the Church, as nothing is known of them in the kingdom of God, many perplexing problems would be solved, and many painful anxieties relieved. It is pitiful, when we come to think about it, that, because of color-prejudices, there should be organized Churches for different races, with all the paraphernalia of denominational appliances. The principles of the Methodist Episcopal Church do not require such an arrangement. Within her pale are some hundreds of thousands of colored people, whose rights are as sacred and as sacredly guarded as are the rights of any other members. It is not, therefore, within us to prefer colored denominational organizations for colored people.

There are, however, three different Churches or denominations of colored Methodists in this country, all in fraternal relations with our own Church. It is not necessary to rehearse the history of these organizations. Each has had some reason for its separate existence. In times past the embarrassments under which the colored people labored were very great. Those who went out from the Methodist Episcopal Church had their grievances—grievances peculiar to that day, and which can never again return. With their disabilities and surroundings, it seemed to them duty to go out, and at this day we dare not say that it was not best. Our present regret is that they are not united in one Church instead of three. The differences between these Churches are not great in principle. They are one in doctrine, as they are one with us; and in Church polity their divergences are comparatively few and insignificant.

Their ultimate aim should be consolidation with the general Methodism of the country. The hand of the Methodist Episcopal Church is extended to each and all of them for fraternity or for organic union. It is not becoming that we press the subject upon them before they desire it. They are committed to the idea of race Churches, and may see in that idea more excellencies than appear to us, accustomed as we are to the larger thought that discards distinctions on race or color lines. In practice there are some advantages in their separation. It brings more men to the front as leaders. It accustoms them to the forms and methods of legislation. But it deprives them of association in this work with others. With some gain, it has many losses.

As a permanent policy it is objectionable on many sides, and for many reasons. In our plan there is all the separation needed. Where they prefer it, the colored people have colored congregations, pastors, and Conferences; yet they are not separated by law or commandment, but for their convenience and comfort. So can it be when all are merged in the one American Methodism.

At the late Ecumenical Conference some steps were taken looking to the union of these three branches of the Church. It will be a great thing for the cause of evangelical Christianity, and for Methodism, and for the colored people, if the African Methodist Episcopal, the African Methodist Episcopal Zion, and the Colored Methodist Church, shall succeed in consolidating their forces. It will be a long stride in the right direction. If they can not come to us, they can do better work as one denomination than as three. Numbers will give them strength. The consolidation will enable them to economize in men and means. It will help eliminate inefficient and unsuccessful preachers. It will enlarge the power of their schools, their publishing agencies, and all their connectional forces. We bid them God-speed! In union among themselves they will be in better condition to consider the ultimate and greater union to which we look in the future, when the broader principles of our own Methodism shall prevail.

It has been said by some that this question of color will be an obstacle in the way of consolidation with the Methodist Episcopal Church, South. It has caused some hesitancy in the past, without doubt. Possibly it may in the future. There is no prejudice that dies harder than color-prejudice.

With our friends in the South the prejudice is not merely against color. Proofs abound that they tolerate color and associate with it, without scruple, when it is kept in servile conditions. It goes hard with them to look upon colored people as other than servile. But they are learning. Southern Methodists are educating the blacks. They have founded one or two schools of good grade for this purpose, and Southern Methodist preachers act as agents for these schools, visiting the Churches, taking collections, and pleading earnestly and eloquently for the education of the colored young men and women of the country.

True, they were late in beginning this work, and they go about it under disadvantages; but they are at it. Revolutions go not backward. They will continue the good work. The seed sown in their Churches will bear fruit. The schools and colleges of our Church in the South have shown such possibilites in this field that the Southern Church could not fail to see duty in a new light, and as the patron of the Colored Methodist Episcopal Church of America she has come to the aid of that Church in educational work in good earnest.

It was widely thought that when the General Conference of the Methodist Episcopal Church, South, organized this colored Church, ordained its bishops, and set it up in independence as a Church, its chief aim was to get rid of its colored membership. There was ground for this thinking. But better things have come to pass. The newly opened fountain of liberality is pouring streams of blessings on the needy. Both Churches are to be congratulated.

The Methodist Episcopal Church, South, is

now the special friend of the colored people—this is her profession. Then why should the fact that there are colored members in the Methodist Episcopal Church, enjoying equal rights under the law of the Church and full representation in the General Conference, be any barrier to the contemplated reunion? When the fraternal delegates from that Church come to our General Conference, and see the colored delegates in their places, taking part in the proceedings and enjoying their liberty, they experience no shock, find no fault, betray no disgust, and suffer no detriment. It can not be that their eloquent strains of fraternal love are intended only for those of light complexion! We have a better opinion of their sincerity and greatness of soul. Their ideas have grown as well as ours. The brotherhood of humanity has dawned upon them with inspiring influence. The gospel of free grace and unbounded redemption in Christ, as preached in their pulpits, gives no uncertain sound, and as the truth is proclaimed that "God is no respecter of persons," those who preach it learn to apply it to the problems and prejudices of the hour. As we believe in the divinity of this gospel, we must believe that all who receive it will ultimately come to the practical recognition of human rights, regardless of race or color.

We will not suffer any suggested doubt of the sincerity of our Southern brethren, in their professions of regard for the colored people, to abide in our hearts. Their education has been different from ours. The old notion that color marked the race for servitude was interwoven with their childhood thoughts, was strengthened by the sights and sounds that greeted their eyes and ears in youth and early life, till it became rooted and grounded in them as next to an ineradicable conviction. It was hard for them to believe in the possibility of educating colored people. Nothing could convince them of this but actual demonstration. The demonstration has come; and the multitudes of colored graduates from our schools and colleges, with refined manners and scholarly bearing, command the approval and admiration of those so recently incredulous as to their capability of education. The revolution is going forward. The Southern people will yet confess the wrongs done to the colored race. They will also cease to be shocked at the idea of recognizing them as brethren in the Church of Jesus Christ.

It is an easy step from the advocacy of the education of young colored people to the acknowledgment of their manhood rights. That step will be taken. It is not a question of social rank, but of the merits of personal character. The Church of God is the first place for the recognition of human rights of every kind. Social equality has never been a condition of the acknowledgment of equal rights under the law of the Church and at the altar of worship. It never can be, except where blinding prejudice obscures all spiritual vision. We can not therefore believe that this question of race is to be a final hindrance to the union of the Churches.

There are excellent qualities in Southern Methodism—qualities worthy of commendation and imitation in all the Churches. Soundness of doctrine is maintained with reference to all that is vital in the Christian system. There is probably less of adventurous speculation in the pulpits of that Church than in our own. The word of God is laid upon the consciences of the people, with its stern requirements and penalties as well as with its promises and grace, as the only standard of moral obligation. This fidelity to the Scriptures as of divine authority, is the saving factor in view of their looser practice of admitting members without probation. A people thoroughly trained in orthodoxy of the Methodist type can not forever hold unworthy views of the rights, the equal rights, of the children of God.

The loyalty of our Southern brethren to denominational interests is worthy of commendation. Their zeal in rebuilding their Church institutions since the desolations of the war has been phenomenal. The history of Methodism scarcely affords a parallel to the successes they have achieved. With untiring industry and singleness of purpose they have wrought, devoting talent and energy to the upbuilding of the cause of God, as they understood it. We have looked admiringly, through the passing years, upon their labor-crowned diligence in restoring the waste places of Zion, and in pushing on victoriously to additional conquests. Having with us a common origin and a common faith,

Southern Methodists have not drifted beyond our sympathy. It delights us to know that they retain, in goodly measure, the characteristics of the older Methodism. The evangelical spirit has not forsaken them. Revivals attend their ministry. The impression prevails, however, that they depend more largely on the pulpit for spiritual work than do some others—more than is good for the spiritual health of the membership. The class-meeting has declined with them more than with us. The prayer-meetings and other social means of grace have less appreciation that they deserve. Nevertheless, we rejoice in the good that remains. Whatever their failure to fill the measure of our ideals of policy and catholicity, we accord them due praise for constancy in trials, and for devotedness to the Methodism of their fathers, and ours.

Rejoicing with them in the tokens of divine approval in their work, and in their prosperity, we scorn to think them wanting in any element of Methodistic loyalty. Far be it from us to suspect that their old-time prejudices will rise to forbid them advancing to the highest standard of Christian liberality. Their horizon is wider than in former years, their faith broader, and we dare believe them in earnest in working for the intellectual and moral uplifting of the colored people. This question of color must in due time solve itself in all the Churches of our Lord.

The trend of the times is for union. Chinese walls of division are scarcely endurable between denominations of different origin and doctrine, much less between those of identical faith. The condition of the country has wonderfully changed since the Church divided. Everything tends to unify the Nation. Slavery is gone, and new conditions prevail. The lines of railroads bind the sections together. Commercial industries have taken on new phases; social life pours through channels hitherto unknown; provincialisms are dying out; the South goes North in summer, and the North goes South in winter.

Sectional interests are being whelmed in the larger interests of the whole people. Why should Methodism lag behind in the forward movement towards the unification? Why should the ghost of slavery thwart the nobler instincts of a people saved of the Lord? Why let the memory of old prejudices destroy the yearnings of Christian love? Why not rise to the height of Christian manhood, and take firm hold of the sublime possibilities of the passing decade, and open the new century with all the hosts of American Methodism in solid column for the conflict with the kingdom of darkness?

The End.

www.ingramcontent.com/pod-product-compliance
Lightning Source LLC
Chambersburg PA
CBHW020143170426
43199CB00010B/863